THE PRESIDENCY

A TRUE BOOK

by
Patricia Ryon Quiri

Children's Press®
A Division of Grolier Publishing
New York London Hong Kong Sydney
Danbury, Connecticut

The White House at night

Reading Consultant
Linda Cornwell
Learning Resource Consultant
Indiana Department
of Education

For Tony Gregorio,
with love from
Mrs. Q.

Visit Children's Press on the Internet at:
http://publishing.grolier.com

Library of Congress Cataloging-in-Publication Data

Quiri, Patricia Ryon.
    The presidency / by Patricia Ryon Quiri.
        p.   cm. — (A true book)
    Includes bibliographical references and index.
    Summary: Examines various aspects of the presidency, providing some
historical background and describing the election, duties, and daily activi-
ties of the president.
    ISBN 0-516-20674-5 (lib. bdg.)   0-516-26438-9 (pbk.)
    1. Presidents—United States—Juvenile literature. [1. Presidents.] I.
Title. II. Series
JK517.Q57 1998
324.6'3'0973—dc21
                                                                              97-48964
                                                                                   CIP
                                                                                    AC

Contents

George Bush

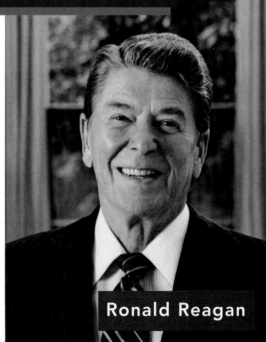
Shirley Chisholm

Each of these individuals tried to become president. Only two of them (Bush and Reagan) succeeded.

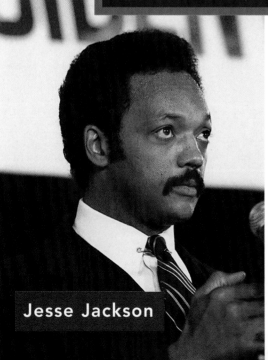
Jesse Jackson

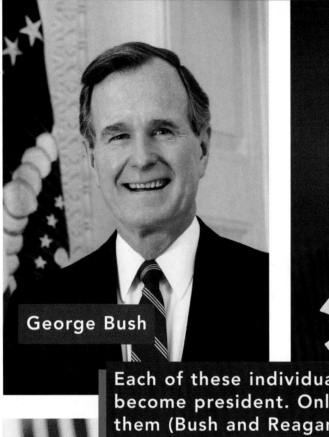
Ronald Reagan

Who Can Be President?

Many boys and girls dream of someday becoming president of the United States. To become president, a person must be elected by the American people. In order to be a candidate for president, there are three basic requirements. First, you must be born a citizen of the United States. Second, you must have lived in the United States for at least fourteen years. And third, you must be at least thirty-five years old.

Although all the presidents of the United States have been white males, women and minorities can run for the office of president, too. Perhaps we will have a woman president in the twenty-first century!

History of the U.S. Government

When the United States of America was very young, representatives, or delegates, from twelve of the thirteen original states got together for a big convention, or meeting. The meeting was held in Philadelphia in 1787.

The Constitutional Convention

It was called the Constitutional
Convention.

The fifty-five delegates
made up the Continental
Congress. The Continental
Congress needed to make a

plan for the new government. They also had to decide who would be the leader of the new government. How much power would he be given? What would he be called?

The Congress asked George Washington to head the Constitutional Convention. Benjamin Franklin, James Madison, and Alexander Hamilton were also at the meeting. It took these men four long, hot months to put together a plan for the government. It was not an easy task. Many times the men disagreed, and there were lots of arguments. Finally, on September 17, 1787, the leaders came to a decision. The plan for the new government was called the United States Constitution.

It took more than two years for all the states to ratify, or accept, the Constitution. Delaware was the first state to do so. Rhode Island was the last.

The inauguration of George Washington, the nation's first President

George Washington was chosen to be the first leader, or president, of the new country. Some people wanted to call him "His Highness, the

President of the United States and Protector of the Rights of the Same." Others thought that title sounded too much like a king.

Finally, it was agreed that Washington would be called president of the United States. The word "president" comes from the word preside, which means to "hold the position of authority." George Washington served as president for eight years, from 1789 to 1797.

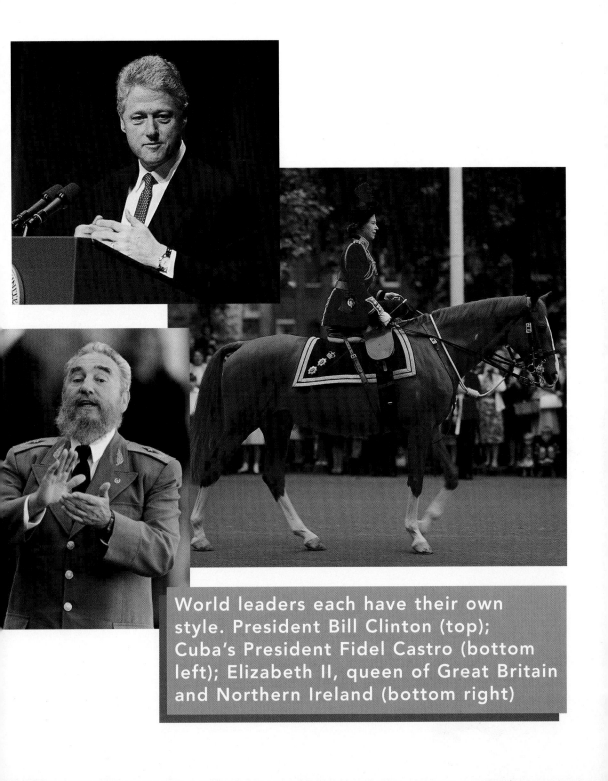

World leaders each have their own style. President Bill Clinton (top); Cuba's President Fidel Castro (bottom left); Elizabeth II, queen of Great Britain and Northern Ireland (bottom right)

How Is the President Elected?

Presidential elections take place every four years in the United States. Voters, such as your parents, grandparents, and other adults, go to the polls. At the polls, citizens vote for the candidate they think should hold office.

Pulling a lever next to a name casts a vote for that person.

Polling places for voting are set up in schools, fire stations, churches, libraries, and other public places.

Election Day is always the first Tuesday in the month of November. In 1996, the presidential election took place on Tuesday, November 5th. Bill Clinton was the incumbent— the current president. He ran against Bob Dole and Ross Perot.

After the people of the United States vote, the Electoral College elects the president. What is the Electoral College? It is a group

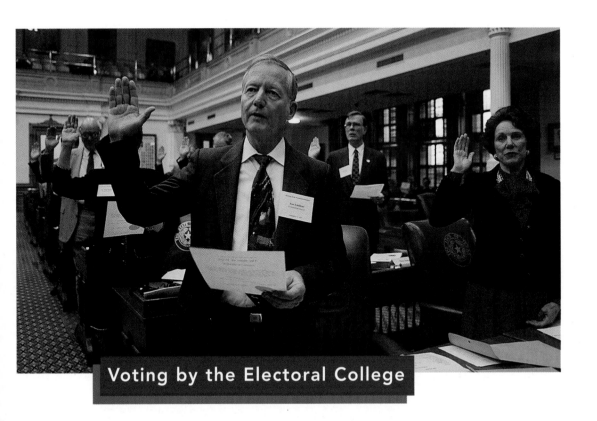

Voting by the Electoral College

of people called electors. They vote for the person that their state voted for. The number of electors from each state is equal to the number of senators and members of the

House of Representatives from that state.

Every state has two senators, but the number of members of the House of Representatives varies for each state. The larger the state's population, the more representatives that state has. For example, California, a large state, has fifty-two repre-sentatives while Vermont, a small state, has only one. So California has fifty-four electors (fifty-two representatives and two senators). And Vermont has three electors (one representative and two senators). You can see why candidates for president always hope to win in the larger states.

To win, a presidential candidate must receive 270 of the 538 electoral votes. Bill Clinton got more electoral votes in 1996 than Bob Dole or Ross Perot, so he was the winner.

A president serves a term of four years. He can be re-elect-

ed for a second term, for a total of eight years. A president may not run again if he has served two terms.

When a new president is elected in November, it takes

time for him and his new staff to get organized. He has about ten weeks between the time of the election and the inauguration. At the inauguration, the president is sworn in. It is a ceremony that formally begins his term in office.

These ten weeks are busy weeks for the president-elect. He must choose people to work for him and organize his staff. He must prepare to move his family to the White House.

The Road to the Presidency

Every four years, the major political parties choose their presidential and vice-presidential candidates at a convention. Then the candidates face weeks of hard work on the campaign trail.

A presidential convention

A campaign speech

They give speeches, take part in debates, and meet as many Americans as possible. Everything comes to an end on Election Day, when the voters go to the polls.

Voters at the polls

The Inauguration

Every president is inaugurated, or sworn in, to office on January 20 at noon, following the election. Thousands of people came to watch the forty-second president of the United States, William Jefferson Clinton, repeat the oath of office outside the Capitol building in Washington, D.C. in 1996.

At President Bill Clinton's inauguration, his daughter Chelsea (left) and wife Hillary (right) look on.

At every inauguration, the president places his left hand on the Bible and raises his right hand. Then he repeats the oath of office:

"I do solemnly swear that I will faithfully execute the Office of President of the United States, and will, to the best of my ability, preserve, protect, and defend the Constitution of the United States."

Who Helps the President?

Being the president of the United States is a very difficult and demanding job. He is in charge of the executive branch of the government. This branch has three parts: the Executive Office of the president, the Cabinet, and the independent agencies.

26

Fortunately, the president has a large staff to help him. Almost two thousand people work for the Executive Office, including advisers and members of government departments.

The people in the president's Cabinet are in charge of government departments. They include the secretary of defense, the secretary of transportation, the secretary of state, and the secretary of

The president (fourth from right) meets with his Cabinet.

education. These people have many others working for them. Cabinet members report directly to the president.

The president also has a personal staff of people who

work in the White House office. The White House is where the president and his family live, and it is also where the president works.

Mike McCurry, President Clinton's press secretary

From His House to the White House

The White House is located at 1600 Pennsylvania Avenue in Washington, D.C. It is a large house with 132 rooms. It was first occupied by President John Adams, who moved there in 1800. For many presidents, the White House is a big change from the homes they lived in when they were young.

From top to bottom: The White House; the birthplace of President John Quincy Adams; boyhood home of President Abraham Lincoln; President Jimmy Carter's boyhood home

What Does the President Do?

Most presidents begin their day by reading the newspapers in the private quarters of the White House. Many times, members of the president's staff have breakfast with him so that they can discuss what is going on that day.

The president works in the Oval Office in the West Wing of

President Reagan often ate his meals and worked at the same time (above). The Oval Office (right)

the White House. The office gets its name from its oval shape. In the Oval Office, the president reads and signs important reports, letters, and papers. Sometimes the president gives speeches from this office, which are broadcast on television.

In the evening, the president and his wife, who is called the First Lady, often entertain guests in the White House.

President Clinton and First Lady Hillary Rodham Clinton entertain the Emperor and Empress of Japan.

Sometimes they just relax by themselves. The White House has a gym, a movie theater, a swimming pool, a tennis court, and a bowling alley.

For getaway weekends, the president and his family may go to Camp David, a vacation home in Maryland. It takes only thirty minutes to get there by helicopter.

The president of the United States is paid a salary of $200,000 a year, as well as $50,000 for expenses. He also gets $100,000 for travel expenses.

The president of the United States has many jobs. He makes sure that the laws of the coun-try are followed. He is also the commander-in-chief of the armed forces, which means that he is in charge of all military actions. However, the president cannot declare war. Only Congress can do that. However, only the president has the authority to use nuclear weapons.

The president can make treaties, or agreements, with other countries, as long as two-thirds of the senators agree

In 1987, President Reagan and Soviet leader Mikhail Gorbachev signed a treaty to ban some nuclear weapons.

with him. The president can tell Congress what laws he would like to see passed, and he can also veto, or reject, laws. However, the Congress has the power to prevent this.

The president often travels to different states and countries. A marine helicopter picks him up on the lawn of the White House and takes him to a special jet called Air Force One. This 747 jet can seat eighty people. It is not like an ordinary plane because it is specially equipped

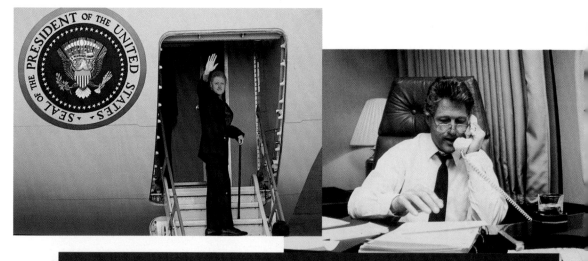

The president boarding Air Force One (left). The President usually doesn't have time to sit back and enjoy the ride. There is always business to be done.

to carry the president, his family, staff, and many reporters. It has a private suite for the president and his family, desks, couches, bedrooms, six bathrooms, and a dining room that can seat up to 100 people.

Who Protects the President?

Four American presidents have been assassinated, or killed, while they were serving their country. After the assassination of President William McKinley in 1901, the Secret Service was given the job of protecting the president and his family.

Bill and Chelsea
Clinton go
shopping,
guarded by
Secret Service
agents (far left
and far right).

The Secret Service is made
up of men and women specially trained as law-enforcement
officers. They protect not only
the president and his family but
also the vice-president and his
family. The president and his
family cannot go anywhere

without the Secret Service. Secret Service agents even guard the president's children while they are in school!

Preserving, protecting, and defending the Constitution of the United States is the job of every president. We, as a nation, vote for the person we feel is right for the good of the country. Perhaps in the next century, you might end up running for this most important office.

◄**T**heodore Roosevelt, the twenty-sixth president, went to Panama in 1906. He was the first president to visit a foreign country.

Franklin D. Roosevelt ▶ was the only president to serve twelve years (1933–1945). He guided the United States through World War II.

Presidents to Remember

John F. Kennedy ▶
was forty-three years
old when he became
President (1961–1963).
He was the youngest
man ever to win the
presidency.

◀ **Richard M. Nixon**
was president from 1969
to 1974. Then a scandal
known as Watergate
forced him to resign
the presidency.

To Find Out More

Here are some additional resources to help you learn more about the President:

 **Books**

Brandt, Keith. **The President.** Troll Associates, 1985.

Brown, Gene. **The 1992 Election.** The Millbrook Press, 1992.

Fradin, Dennis B. **Voting and Elections.** Children's Press, 1985.

Quiri, Patricia Ryon. **The Congress.** Children's Press, 1998.

Quiri, Patricia Ryon. **The Supreme Court.** Children's Press, 1998.

Spies, Karen. **Our Presidency.** The Millbrook Press, 1994.

Organizations and Online Sites

Abraham Lincoln Online
http://www.netins.net/ showcase/creative/lincoln. html

Everything about Lincoln, from his writings to the places he lived in

The First Lady's Home Page
http://www.whitehouse.gov/ WH/EOP/First_Lady/html/ HILLARY_Home-plain.html

The First Lady's biography, speeches, photo scrap-book, and more

Inaugural Addresses of the Presidents
http://www.columbia.edu/ acis/bartleby/inaugural/ index.html

Speeches of every president, from Washington to Bush

Mount Rushmore National Memorial Society
P.O. Box 1524
Rapid City, SD 57709

Books and information on the famous memorial that shows the faces of four great presidents

Uncle Sam for Kids!
www.win.org/library/mtls/ govdocs/kids.htm

A wide range of links about government and politics

Welcome to the White House for Kids
http://www.whitehouse.gov/ WH/kids/html/home.html

A tour of the White House with Socks the cat

White House Historical Association
740 Jackson Place NW
Washington, DC 20503

Offers education to increase our understanding and enjoyment of the White House

Important Words

assassinate to kill

Cabinet advisers to the President who head government departments

Constitution plan of government by which the country is ruled

convention large meeting of the members of a political party

delegate individual chosen to represent a group

election voting people into office

Electoral College group of people who make the final choice of president

inauguration formal beginning of the president's term in office

incumbent person who is currently in office

ratify accept

veto reject

Index

Meet the Author

Patricia Ryon Quiri lives in Palm Harbor, Florida, with her husband Bob and three sons. She is a graduate of Alfred University in upstate New York and has her degree in elementary education. Ms. Quiri currently teaches elementary school in the Pinellas County School system. Other books by Ms. Quiri include a five-part series on American landmarks and symbols, five books in the U.S. government series, and other books for Children's Press.

DUE